The Alsace Wine Route, or Route des Vins, is a winding ribbon of flower-bedecked villages stretching 170 kilometres from Thann in the south, to Cleebourg in the north of Alsace. Founded some 50 years ago in 1953, the route takes visitors through the heart of the Alsace winemaking country, where winemakers have been toiling in the vineyards since back in Roman times. This expertise, handed down through the ages, is responsible for some of the world's finest wines, to be found in these picturesque villages that dot the route, with their half-timbered houses and marvellously authentic restaurants, monuments to the tradition of Alsace gastronomy. This guide is designed to help you find your way along the wine route and experience for yourself the multiple pleasures of Alsace at its finest.

A noted tourist attraction, the Alsace Wine Route is above all the expression of a thousand years of expertise.

A short history of Alsace wine

The vineyards of Alsace are considered to be among the oldest in France and their history can be traced back over twenty centuries. The Route des Vins, or Wine Route, as we know it today, was created some 50 years ago, in 1953. The vineyards have experienced all the trials and tribulations, the ups and downs and the triumphs and disasters of Alsace and have won themselves a reputation as one of the truly great wine-producing regions of both France and the world. The first vines were cultivated in Roman times, when legionnaires, weary from their litany of conquests, decided to settle and devote themselves to more peaceful pursuits, including the production of wine.

A drastic brake was put on vineyard expansion in 92 AD when the Emperor Domitian banned planting, following prolonged overproduction in Europe. It was not until the late 11th century, under the Merovingian and Carolingian kings, that the wine industry began to develop, reaching its first golden age around the 16th century.

The Thirty Years War (1618 – 1648) spelt disaster for both Alsace and its wine, and after the destruction wrought by the war (along with sudden changes in the climate of the time), it took an enormous amount of time and effort for the wine-producers' guilds to get the vines up and growing again. However, it was not until the French Revolution, and the disappearance of the guilds that the industry was able to re-organise itself and update its structures.

By the 19th century, the spirit of liberalism was leading wine-producers to plant their vines willy-nilly, using any kind of varietal that caught their fancy and vinifying the wine in what they thought was the ideal way, having been taught by Napoleon's minister of agriculture, Jean-Antoine Chaptal, that sugar increased the degree of alcohol in the wine and by Doctor Gall that the best way of making a good wine lay in adding water, which brought acidity down.

The practice of labelling the bottle with the grape variety as well as the name of the region began in Alsace in 1919. Sylvaner, Riesling, Gewurztraminer and Pinot Noir rapidly achieved prominence. In 1945, freed of the German occupation, Alsace wine obtained its first appellation d'origine, in an edict signed by General de Gaulle. Alsace winemakers were aware of the increasing demand for quality wines and moved to improve their production. Their efforts were rewarded in 1962, when Vin d'Alsace was promoted to the rank of AOC (appellation d'origine contrôlée), although by then the number of permitted grape varieties in the region had been cut to eleven. The new status meant a limitation in the size of the vines and a progressive reduction in maximum permitted yield (130 hl in 1983, 88 hl in 2000).

The winemaker breathes in the bouquet of the wine, the fruit of his labour.

The "Typicité" of Alsace wines

Alsace has traditionally made dry, white wines, with Pinot Noir the odd grape out, used for making rosé or red, according to the vinification, the vintage and the use or not of oak casks. Alsace wines are renowned for the richness and complexity of their aromas, properties that are directly related to the type of grape varieties grown in the region. The direction in which the vines face (often south and south-east) will also have a significant effect on the maturity of the grapes, which is one of the main reasons why the vineyards with the best exposure to the sun have been well known since the Middle Ages.

A major step forward was taken in 1975, with the official establishment of the Alsace Grand Cru appellation, which included 50 terroirs, producing the finest wines in Alsace.

Two major requirements

The AOC qualification requires Alsace winemakers to follow two other major directives.
• <u>Firstly,</u> Alsace wines could only be bottled in the slender, usually green-coloured "Flûte d'Alsace".
• <u>Secondly,</u> the wines had to be bottled within the production area.

The Wine Route

The wine villages
& characteristics of the terroirs

The Alsace vineyard stretches from Thann at the bottom of the region, to Marlenheim in the North (not forgetting Cleebourg isolated right up at the top of the region), a hundred or so kilometres along the approaches to the Vosges. The vines are planted on the foothills, around a multitude of ancestral villages, bursting with charm.

All the charm of a typical winemaker's house.

Winemaker's houses

Alsatian houses have the picturesque charm that makes them a major attraction for visitors to the region. Those built by the winemakers along the Wine Route occupy a place of their own. Often brightly coloured and bedecked with flowers, they can usually be identified by the densely-packed beams of their half-timbered facades. You will often find skilfully incorporated Gothic, Roman and Baroque styles, with richly-carved windows featuring religious and other scenes or with a date, names or a family maxim, that will reveal the date they were built, along with the religion and status of the occupants. A number of houses will also have a sundial or a tree of life on the beams. In Molsheim, Traenheim, Nordheim, Ribeauvillé, Kaysersberg and Riquewihr, the ground floor is made of simple brickwork, whereas the upper floors are half-timbered, while Mittelbergheim is dominated by vast wine-producers' farmhouses, not unlike those to be found in Eguisheim and Gueberschwihr, that date back to the 16th and 18th centuries. In the courtyards, the cellar will be at a level below the living quarters and will house a wine press, sometimes richly decorated in the same style as the great wooden barrels, or tuns, that line the cellar walls.

Thann

The southern gateway to the wine route, Thann is home to the Rangen Grand Cru. Drop by the Tour des Sorcières (Witches' Tower) to find out all about the town and the vineyards of Alsace. There is an exhibition giving an over-view of the terroirs as well as their geology and a description of how the wine producers do their job.

Not to be missed : The pride of the town is the Saint-Thiébaut collegial church (13th / 16th centuries), made of pink sands-tone, situated next to the town fortifications, themselves built in 1360 and guarded by the Tour des Sorcières (Witches' tower) and the Tour des Cigo-gnes (Storks' Tower). The local museum, the musée des Amis de Thann in the old cornhall and the Renaissance Cabane des Bagnards (a type of prison) are also worth seeing, along with the fountains of Saint-Thiébaut and the Vignerons (winemakers) and the ruins of the château d'Engelbourg with its stone eye.

There are only 19 ha of land under vine around Thann, but it was the only site in Alsace to be entirely classified Grand Cru. Grand Cru Rangen has a unique volcanic soil which produces fruity Rieslings and full-bodied Pinot Gris and Gewurztraminers of great elegance and breeding.

Thann, the southern gateway to the Wine Route.

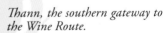

Leimbach

The village of Leimbach, perched at the southern most tip of the Alsace vineyard, is worth visiting for the 18th century St. Blaise church, with its Roman entrance, the "Auf der Heiden" chapel of Notre Dame, built in the 15th century and the St. Blaise reliquary, displayed in the new church.

The wine villages stretch out along the route, like pearls of wine

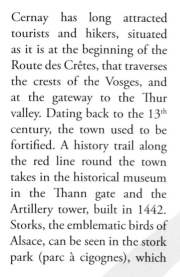

Vieux Thann

Dating back further than its homonymous sister-village, Vieux-Thann's vines are also part of the Rangen Grand Cru. Don't miss St. Dominique's church, built in the 12th century with the final embellishments added in the 18th century.

Cernay

Cernay has long attracted tourists and hikers, situated as it is at the beginning of the Route des Crêtes, that traverses the crests of the Vosges, and at the gateway to the Thur valley. Dating back to the 13th century, the town used to be fortified. A history trail along the red line round the town takes in the historical museum in the Thann gate and the Artillery tower, built in 1442. Storks, the emblematic birds of Alsace, can be seen in the stork park (parc à cigognes), which borders a signposted discovery trail round the Thur and a similarly waymarked mining trail around the old iron mines of Erzenbach, while a third trail, the circuit des oratories, also signposted, takes visitors on a walk round the local shrines. For the sport-inclined, there is a mountain-bike track and a hiking trail, while rail buffs can take the Doller tourist train.

Uffholtz

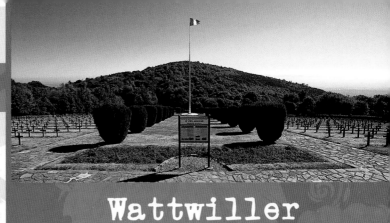

Uffholtz contains the ruins of the 14th century mediaeval château, the Herrenfluh, as well as a number of Rennaissance houses and a chapel dedicated to St. Anthony. A sign of more recent events is the First World War memorial.

Wattwiller

Wattwiller has been famous for its spa waters ever since Roman times and can also boast a healthy wine-making heritage, as witnessed by its old title of provostship of the Abbey of Murbach, attested with the seigniorial vineyard. Not to be missed: The 15th century St. John-the-Baptist church and the remains of the foundations, built in 1260 and which remind us of the town's turbulent history, as illustrated by the Vieil-Armand necropolis (1914-18) and the nearby Hartmannwillerkopf hill, site of fierce fighting in 1915.

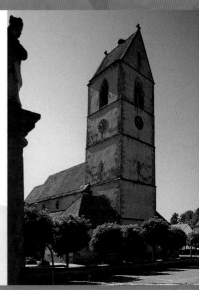

Grand Cru

Wuenheim

Wuenheim is also close to the Vieil-Armand mountain, known too as the Hartmannwillerkopf. The village has a Grand Cru, the Ollwiller, named after its eponymous château, a winemaking museum (cave viticole du Vieil Armand) and a wine trail.
The elevation of Ollwiller to Grand Cru status brought this previously little-known site more into prominence. Suitable notably for Riesling and Gewurztraminer, it produces elegant wines of some subtlety.

Soultz

Soultz is a military town that once boasted 3 castles and 18 turrets to keep its inhabitants safe. Sights include the tour des Remparts (Ramparts tower), the 17th / 19th century Château d'Anthés and the residence of the Commander of the Order of St. John of Malta, with its "Nef des Jouets" (Nave of Toys).

Among the other buildings of note, look for the 14th / 17th century Bucheneck museum, splendid Renaissance-style houses and the 18th century Hôtel de Ville (Town Hall). Situated in the extreme south of the Haut Rhin, Soultz offers an easy-drinking, well-balanced Pinot Blanc along with a cheerful Riesling with pleasant aromas.

Grand Cru

Guebwiller

Guebwiller is overlooked by the Grand Ballon, at 1424m the highest of the Vosgian peaks. The town is dominated by its three churches, the 12ᵗʰ century St. Leger, the 18ᵗʰ century Notre Dame and the 14ᵗʰ century Dominican convent, now used as a music and culture centre. Considered as one of the region's main wine-production centres, Guebwiller possesses four of Alsace's finest Grands Crus, more than any other town or village in Alsace. Spiegel, possibly the least known, produces Riesling of delicate bouquet; the Saering Grand Cru also produces excellent floral, fruity Rieslings and muscats, while Kessler's Gewurtztraminers are spicy and mellow. The fourth Grand Cru, Kitterlé, is famous for its Rieslings of great finesse and mellow, gently-rich Gewurtz-traminers and Pinot Gris. Come along in May and taste the whole lot at the Guebwiller annual wine fair.

Grand Cru

Bergholtz

Curled up at the foot of the Spiegel Grand Cru, Bergholtz possesses an 18ᵗʰ century church as well as the remnants of the Vauban canal that used to carry stone from the imposing old quarries of Vosges sandstone. Taste the suavely elegant Gewurztraminer and do not miss the fine, racy Rieslings and the full-bodied Pinot Gris, especially those grown in the Spiegel vineyards, which also run over into neighbouring Guebwiller.

Bergholtz-Zell

The vestiges of an 11th century sanctuary, consecrated by Alsace's only Pope, St. Leo XI, are to be found in the church, while the garden and 19th century calvary of Oelberg, with its full-size polychrome wood Last Supper, shows the village's strong religious antecedents. Although not as well known as its neighbouring villages, Bergholtz-Zell produces racy wines of high quality.

Grand Cru

Orschwihr

An ancient fief of the Hapsburgs, in the 12th, 15th and 18th centuries, the remains of the mediaeval manor and the château of Settenberg can still be seen, along with the 16th century church tower, splendid Renaissance houses and a well dating back to 1766. The village is bounded by the Bollenberg (hitherto famous for its witches and now for its protected flora), the Lippelsberg and the Pfingstberg Grand Cru. The signposted wine trail will take you through the vines, following which you should taste the excellent Rieslings and crisp, dry Muscat. Pfingstberg gives highly individual wines with a marked floral character, that can be kept for long years.

Soultzmatt

Soultzmatt is situated at the foot of the region's highest Grand Cru, the Zinnkoepflé (420 metres altitude), with its steep, rugged slopes that produce luscious, spicy Gewurtztraminers and excellent Rieslings and Pinot Gris. Part of the Zinnkoepflé is located within the commune of Westhalten and a wine trail will take you around the vines. The village's annual wine fair is held on the first Saturday of August.

Château Wagenbourg

A beauty spot of the Noble Valley well worth visiting, Soultzmatt is famous both for its wine and its water – the village is home to the Lisbeth eau de source and Nessal mineral water. Other sights to see include the St. Sebastian church (12th, 15th and 18th centuries), the château of Wagenbourg and the Val de Pâtre chapel.

Westhalten

Westhalten is located at the beginning of the Noble Valley and its flourishing vineyards produce charming Sylvaner and excellent Pinot Blanc. The village's Rieslings often have plant aromas with a supple, slightly feminine side, while the Gewurztraminers show a delicate structure of some distinction. Westhalten shares the Vorbourg Grand Cru with Rouffach and Zinnkoepflé with Soultzmatt and also edges into the Steinert Grand Cru. The village also possesses a number of well-known lieux-dits, the Lutzelberg, Strangen-berg, Bollenberg and Sundel, which can be seen if you take the well-marked botanical wine trail, bordered by splendid Mediterranean flora.

Vorbourg and Zinnkoepflé, two of the Grand Crus that are the pride of the Wine Route

Grand Cru

Rouffach

Rouffach has some fine Renaissance houses in the Place de la République and is also renowned for its witches, the memory of whom is cele-brated each year at the foot of their 12th century tower. It is also worth spending some time going round the Notre Dame church (13th – 16th century), the

Eglise des Récollets (Friars' Church) and the historical museum, walking round the ramparts and taking the wine trail. At Ascension weekend, thousands of people pour into the village for the annual organic produce fair. Rouffach has long been known for its wines, especially the Vorbourg Grand Cru. The village enjoys a micro-climate that favours Riesling, Gewurztraminer, Pinot Gris and Muscat, while the Vorbourg Grand Cru produces full-bodied wines that keep well and possess considerable finesse.

Pfaffenheim

Lying under the splendid view offered by the shrine of Notre Dame of Schauenberg, Pfaffenheim contains a number of lovely wine-producers' houses and a church with a 13th century chancel. A wine trail takes visitors on a walk round the vines. The Fête des Caves the second weekend in July, brings the crowds in for two days of fun and wine-tasting. The Pinot Blanc has a fine reputation and tasters can sometimes catch a hint of musk in the mouth. The Riesling and Gewurztraminer can also be excellent. The village possesses the little-known, limestone-based Steinert Grand Cru on whose steep slopes grow the vines that produce Gewurztraminer, Pinot Gris and Riesling with highly developed aromas.

Gueberschwihr

A village which, while slightly off the main tourist tracks, possesses wines whose well-defined personality certainly merit close attention. The Muscats are delicious and bursting with fruit. Guebers-chwihr boasts a superb 19th century church with a three-storey 12th-century tower that looms over Merovingian sarcophagi, a bridge and 16th century houses.

A wine trail allows visitors to explore the vineyards, while the village's wine-producers throw open their doors on the last weekend of August for the annual wine fair. Gueberschwihr's Grand Cru, the Goldert, produces deeply-coloured, flavour-packed Gewurztraminers and Muscats, not to mention Riesling and Pinot Gris.

Gueberschwihr has provided the backdrop for several films.

Hattstatt

Hattsatt shares the Hatschbourg Grand Cru with neighbouring Voegtlinshoffen, and the heavy soil provides excellent conditions for Gewurztraminer, Pinot Gris and Riesling, all of which can be examined by taking the village's wine trail. Hattsatt also has a 12th century church with a Roman nave, a 14th century Gothic chancel and 15th century wooden sculptures, along with a 16th century Town Hall and a number of old houses.

Herrlisheim

Have a look within the village walls at the fortified tower dating back to 1370, the church with its 14th century Gothic steeple and lateral chapel and its sculptured doorways. The village has a wine trail and the Fête de la Grenouille (Frog Festival) on the last weekend of June.

Obermorschwihr

Obermorschwihr's church has a splendid 15th century half-timbered church tower, while visitors should also have a look round the remains of the Augustine abbey of Marbach, built in the 12th century, only to fall into ruin in the 18th century, three centuries after its apogee in the 15th century. The monks of the abbey showed such skill in tending the vines that the wine won itself a reputation recorded in one journal as "in the lieu-dit "Masel", there matures a wine that is the best from Wissembourg to Basel". The village's Muscat and Gewurztraminer can still rival with the finest of the neighbouring villages.

Vœgtlinshoffen

Voegtlinshoffen is famous primarily for the crisp, fruit-packed excellence of its Muscats, which, in the Hatschbourg Grand Cru, can attain a quality rarely achieved elsewhere. The annual wine festival in the last weekend

of June is a great opportunity to drink the Muscat and the other wines of the village, while admiring the church with its altar from the Capuchin convent in Colmar and its 18th-century-style furniture.

Husseren-les-Châteaux

The village of Husseren-les-Châteaux lies under the three châteaux of Eguisheim and, at 390 m, is the highest point of the wine route. The 12th century baptismal rear of the church was brought in from the abandoned abbey of Murbach. In July and August, the village organises a special walk around the village and its surroundings, with their exceptional view over the plain of Alsace and the Black Forest, including a tour of the vines and a tasting session. Husseren-les-Châteaux produces top-quality wines, with Pinot Gris and Gewurztraminer enjoying particularly high reputations.

Eguisheim

Fortified château, place du Château Saint-Léon.

Eguisheim, with its clay-limestone soil, produces a wonderfully drinkable Pinot Blanc, full-bodied Rieslings, luscious Gewurztraminers and one of the best-balanced Muscats in Alsace. The Eichberg Grand Cru enjoys a micro-climate that favours Riesling, Gewurztraminer and Pinot Gris, producing highly fruity wines of

considerable finesse. The village's second Grand Cru, the Pfersig-berg, with its calcareous marl and limestone soil gives full-bodied, fruity, long-lived Gewurztraminer and fine, rich, elegant Riesling, Pinot Gris and Muscat. Eguisheim is a mediaeval village, with three ruined châteaux perched on the heights above Husseren-les-Châteaux and is one of the prettiest of the Alsace wine route. The village was blessed by Pope Leo XI, the Alsatian Pope, and was built in three concentric circles around the château, where the future Pope was born in 1002. Eguisheim provides an excellent example of how military and civilian architecture can be harmoniously blended. Highlights include a church with a Roman tympanum, a 13th century steeple and a polychrome wood Virgin Mary with arms outstretched. Walk round the village to see the remains of the Roman castle, the many old, half-timbered houses, tithe cour-tyards, balconies, oriel windows, fountains and gables that make up the charm of Eguisheim. A wine trail with guided tours and a full tasting and the Wine Festival in the fourth weekend in August make the village a magnet for wine lovers.

Wettolsheim

Guarded by the nearby ruins of the 13th century château of Hagueneck, Wettolsheim is the first wine village from the top of the Haut Rhin, producing well-made, nicely-balanced wines. The village has its own Grand Cru, the Steingrubler, ideally suited to the Riesling in the upper part, and Gewurztraminer on the richer ground of the lower slopes. These opulent, full-bodies wines offer a vast planet of aromas and are the pride and joy of the annual wine festival, held in the last weekend of July.

Don't forget to taste the wines from the lieux-dits Leimenthal, Rosenberg and Kruett.

Wintzenheim

At Wintzenheim are to be found wines marked by the hands of their makers and with their own particular character. The Pinot Blancs slip down nicely, while the Muscat is a revelation. The local Grand Cru, the Hengst (meaning "stallion") is one of the best known in Alsace and gives marvellously expressive Gewurztraminer, Riesling and Pinot Gris. Drunk young, Hengst wines already show untamed complexity and an excellent propensity for ageing. The village of Wintzenheim nestles in the shadow of the châteaux of Hohlandsbourg and Pflixbourg (13th century), on the route des Cinq Châteaux. Although the village is not the most exciting in Alsace, visitors can find vestiges of a 1st – 5th century Roman villa discovered on a slope of the Hengst and an 18th century fountain, before going on to admire the façade of the Changala bakery with its pretty polychrome naïve decoration.

Zimmerbach

This village produces fresh, typically zesty wines that are mostly to be found under the name of the vineyard of Côtes du Val Saint-Grégoire. It is situated at the head of the valley of Munster, famous for its pungent cheese, and is bordered with disused copper mines. The more active-minded can venture along the attractive sports trail that runs across vines and woods.

St. George's church.

27

Walbach

Walbach is between Zimmerbach and Wihr-au-Val and possesses a neo-classical church and a 16th century château. Don't miss the excellent wines of the Felsen lieu-dit.

Wihr-au-Val

A mystic village with a 15th century ossuary chapel dedicated to St. Michael and a stations of the cross with an 18th century chapel, Wihr-au-Val marks the end of the vineyards in the Munster Valley.

Grand Cru

Turckheim

Turckheim long ago made itself a name for its wines. The granite soils of the Brand, the local Grand Cru, produces superb Riesling, Pinot Gris and Gewurztraminer. Wines from the Brand first won renown in the Middle Ages and possess great finesse and subtlety, with a fruity persistence and a marvellous balance.

Turckheim was made an Imperial town back in 1354 and offers the visitor some highly enjoyable sightseeing. There still remain the vestiges of the old ramparts, with the France,

Brand and Munster Gates and the Ste Anne church (1190) with its tower cum entrance. Splendid Renaissance and half-timbered houses with oriel windows and decorated balconies line the streets, while the well-designed historical trail will also take you to the 16th century Corps de Garde (guardroom) and 18th century fountain. Not to be missed, the nocturnal round of the Nightwatchman, that starts at 10 pm, May through to October. A signposted wine trail takes visitors around the vines above the town to enjoy the sumptuous viewpoints (guided tours and tastings are always available). The Wine Festival on the first weekend of August is a must.

The Turkheim nightwatchman.

Grand Cru

Niedermorschwihr

Nestled in the middle of the hills behind Turkheim, Niedermorschwihr produces some remarkable wines, including the Sommerberg Grand Cru, with its steep slopes (45°) and granite soil. The Riesling is exceptionally elegant, especially after a few years in the cellar. Superb, well-defined Pinot Gris and Gewurztraminer are also well worth the effort. Niedermorschwihr is noteworthy for its church topped with a twisted steeple, the only one of its kind in Alsace, and its 13th century chancel. The village also has a number of fine old houses with oriel windows, while visitors should hurry to taste the delicious jams, the best in Alsace, made by Christine Ferber.

Ingersheim

Home to the Florimont Grand Cru where Gewurztraminer is the star, but which also produces excellent, well-balanced Riesling, Muscat and Pinot Gris which will mature well. The Ingersheim wine cooperative can boast the largest wooden wine-barrel in Alsace, with a capacity of 354 hectolitres. The main attractions of the village are its baroque-style church with Roman and Gothic influences and an onion church-tower and the nearby 13th century tour des Sorcières (Witches tower).

Old Renaissance town hall.

The Koifhus, or old customs house, and the Schwendi fountain. Place de l'Ancienne Douane.

Colmar is the wine capital of Alsace and certainly one of the most picturesque towns in the region, offering the visitor a vast choice of sights to enjoy. The town's five museums include the Unterlinden with its world-famous Retable of Issenheim by Mathias Grünewald, a masterpiece of religious art. The old part of the town is pedestrianised and you can spend many happy hours wandering around the Petite Venise and the Tanners districts, admiring the numerous mediaeval churches, especially the St.Martin collegiate church, which contains the Virgin at the Rose Bush,

painted by Martin Schongauer in 1473. Rest weary legs while having a drink or a meal at one of the town's excellent restaurants.

Colmar has its own International Classical Music Festival (first two weeks in July), along with a major wine festival (week of 15th August), Nativity celebrations and four Christmas markets (from late November to late December). The CIVA, the professional body representing Alsace wine, has its headquarters in Colmar.

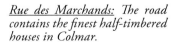

Rue des Marchands: *The road contains the finest half-timbered houses in Colmar.*

Katzenthal

Sheltered within a small valley, Katzenthal, literally "cat valley", possesses a soil that is ideal for the Riesling grape. The village is home to the Sommerberg Grand Cru, one of the finest in all Alsace. An attractive geological trail takes visitors on a trip around the geomorphology of the Vosges and the various rocky structures that make up its subsoil. The château of Wineck, built amid the vine-filled slopes leading down to the village, offers an imposing defensive wall behind which looms out of the rocks a Roman keep of square design, built in around 1200. The keep was extended upwards in the 14th century, and has been preserved through the care and attention of a dynamic association of friends of the château. In winter 1944, the village found itself right in the middle of the battle for the Colmar pocket and was almost completely destroyed. The building work carried out after the war restored Katzenthal to its former charm.

Wine-lovers can also have a taste of two Katzentahl wines made from an blend of grape varieties, the Gentil Katz and the Voyou de Katz.

Ammerschwihr

Ammerschwihr nestles within a series of west-facing hills that roll down to within the outskirts of the village. It has the largest area of vines in Alsace, including the Kaefferkopf, a hill where the vines that make some of the finest wines in the region are grown. This attractive, wine-producing town grew steadily in size throughout the Middle Ages. Vestiges that remain today include the Fripons or knaves' tower and the Bourgeois tower. The town prospered until the Second World War, but suffered heavy damage in the attacks of December 1944. Since reconstructed, visitors can still admire the wild man fountain (fontaine de l'homme sauvage), as well as the Renaissance-style carved door that used to give onto the old town hall, some splendid 16th century houses, the late-Gothic style St. Martin's church with its monumental Christ on the cross, representative of popular religious art of the late 15th century and its Renaissance stairway leading to the gallery, along with the High gate (porte Haute) at the western entrance to the town with its 13th century half-timbered tower and sundials painted on each side and topped with the stork's nest that gives it its name. A couple of steps away is the old seat of the wine-makers guild, housed within an opulent 16th century building.

Visitors can also walk around a vine garden and learn about all the grape varietals to be found in Alsace, along with a sample group of the fruit trees grown in the region. The first wine festival of the year, is held in Ammerschwihr in the last weekend in April, while the Vinogast Wine Fair takes place twice-yearly, in April and November. The only one of its kind in Alsace, a spectacular 18-hole public golf course runs along the road to Labaroche, covering some 60 hectares. The town produces a refreshingly dry Chasselas, Riesling of undeniable breeding and a delicately rich Gewurztraminer that needs a least a year in the bottle to begin to bring out its hidden charms.

The 13th century gateway houses a stork's nest.

Kaysersberg

A jewel of Mediaeval architecture built in the narrow Weiss valley, Kaysersberg is a village of singular beauty. Its wines, made from grapes picked from the slopes bordering the village are marked by a high level of aromatic concentration, notably with the full-bodied Rieslings and Gewurtztraminers, both of which will improve after a few years in the cellar.

Kaysersberg was once an Imperial free town and offers a seductive blend of Middle Ages and Renaissance architecture that gives it an unrivalled charm. Among the whole litany of places to visit in the village, do not miss the 12th century church, with its 16th century retable, the imposing 13th century château, the Renaissance Hôtel de Ville (Town Hall), the fortified bridge and the towers that used to be part of the fortifications. Kaysersberg has a long

history of humanism and is the birthplace of Nobel peace prize winner Albert Schweizer. The Schweitzer museum is located in the house where the "good doctor" was born. Kaysersberg is also home to the most authentic of Alsace's Christmas markets, an ideal opportunity to taste a local specialty, the Bière des Vignes, flavoured with marc de Gewurztraminer.

Kientzheim

Kientzheim originally belonged to the Counts of Lupfen and obtained its urban status and the right to build a rampart in 1430. The town was also once home to the Knights of the Order of Malta and was bought in 1563 by baron Lazare de Schwendi, an imperial diplomat and general, who built the eponymous château. Legend (and only legend) relates that it was Lazare de Schwendi who introduced the Tokay grape to France after a campaign in Hungary… Lazare is closely associated with the local wine tradition as it is within the château walls that the meetings of the venerable Saint Etienne brotherhood of winemakers are held and the museum of Alsace Wine and Vines (musée du Vignoble et des Vins d'Alsace) housed. Kientzheim came back to France under Louis XIV and would belong to Colmar right up to the Revolution. The St. Felix and Ste. Régula chapel attracted large numbers of

At the western entrance to the town there is the château of Reich von Reichenstein, which was severely damaged in the fighting of 1944 and restored by the town according to the architectural canons of the 18th century. The original fortified gate to Kaysersberg has disappeared and visitors now leave the town past a thousand-year-old oak tree and under the steely eye of a Sherman tank, nicknamed "Le Renard", or The Fox, a reminder of the fierce fighting in 1944/45 that led up to the Liberation of Alsace. The place du Lieutenant Robert Dutilh, dedicated to heroes of the Resistance, leads to the vineyards that spread out behind the town. Once past the Schneckentor or Törel pedestrian gate, visitors will find themselves under plane trees that shade the charming fountain from which begins the walking tour round the town and the wine trail that goes through the local Schlossberg and Furstentum grand crus. Schlossberg extends above both the Kientzheim and Kaysersberg communes and its steep slopes produce Riesling, Pinot Gris, Gewurztraminer and Muscat of great concentration and extract. Furstentum is also extremely steep (37°) and the Riesling, Pinot Gris and Gewurztraminer made from its grapes can show great finesse and remarkable aromatic concentration.

pilgrims in the 13th century and now contains a noteworthy collection of 15th century statues, a number of often moving thanksgiving plaques and a rare yellow sandstone sepulchre dated 1490.

The Confrérie Saint Etienne and the Vine Museum !

The Wine Museum ! The château of Lazare de Schwendi has been owned by the Confrérie Saint Etienne, or Herrenstuben-gesellschaft (Company of Gentlemen) as it was called by the Ammerschwihr town council, since 1973. The Confrérie (or brotherhood of winemakers) works to enhance the reputation and quality of Alsace wines. The château contains a remarkable oenotheque, but only the outhouses can be visited. These contain a museum with three floors of exhibitions on the art and techniques of winemaking over the centuries. The museum provides an active link between the present day and the last thousand years and presents a spectacular homage to those winemakers who have toiled to make the Alsace route des vins the undisputed success and road of excellence that it is today. The museum is open every day from June to September, from 10 a.m. to 12 a.m. and from 2 p.m. to 6 p.m.

Grand Cru
Sigolsheim

Winemaking on the Sigolsheim hillsides can traced back to Merovingian times and the only wine to rival the local production was that of Falerna, the finest Southern Italy could offer. Sigolsheim's wines still enjoy a considerable reputation, starting with the Mambourg grand cru, with its predeliction for Gewurztraminer but also planted with Pinot Gris, Muscat and Riesling giving wines of considerable elegance, power and aging potential. The vines can be inspected at close quarters by following the signposted wine trail. Sigolsheim first became known back in the 8th century and has since had its fair share of ups and downs, culminating in its near destruction during the battle of the Colmar pocket in winter 1944. The village is dominated by the sinister-sounding blutberg or blood mountain, a reminder of the fierceness of the combats. A national necropolis stands on top of the hill, with gravestones commemorating 1684 French and American soldiers who fell in the fighting. The lovingly-restored 12th century church of St. Paul and St. Peter, which

managed to get through the destruction largely unscathed, rises proudly above the village. The church is a superb example of the southern-Rhine Romanesque art of the period, its cold beauty giving out an impression of strength and stability. The decoration of the western façade and the central doorway are well worth seeing. A monastery built on the remains of the Oberhof houses a congregation of moniales, perpetuating the tradition of mysticism that has long been an integral part of the village. The Oberhof was given by Charlemagne to the abbey of Ebermunster and confirmed by his son Louis the Debonair in 817. It was demolished during the Revolution and has been run by the Poor Clare capuchin nuns since 1951.

Bennwihr

Since its total destruction in the Second World War bombings, Bennwihr has managed to regain its position in Alsace's wine rankings. Its monumental pink sandstone fountain, dedicated to Ste Odile, is well worth a look, while its wine trail stretches through the Marckrain Grand Cru, known for its powerfully aromatic, full-bodied Gewurztraminer and Pinot Gris. Bennwihr's wine festival is held on the second weekend in August.

Mittelwihr

Like neighbouring Bennwihr, Mittelwihr was destroyed in the winter fighting of 1944-45. Its Mandelberg Grand Cru is bounded by almond trees growing along the wine trail. Mandelberg is reputed for the excellence and delicacy of its Gewurztraminer, Riesling and Muscat.

Beblenheim

Beblenheim is ovelooked by the Sonnenglanz Grand Cru, in 1935 the second vineyard in Alsace to be officially defined. The village also produces a Sylvaner with a good bouquet and an elegant Riesling that will keep well. The village is also the birthplace of the famous ampelographer Chrétien Oberlin, whose work on grape varieties made a major contribution to improving the local vines.

Beblenehim wine cooperative.

Riquewihr

Riquewihr is a marvellous mixture of Mediaeval and Renaissance styles that has long made it a must for any visitor to Alsace. Jean Jacques Waltz, better known as the illustrator and cartoonist Hansi, was born here and his old house is now given over to a museum celebrating the unique talents of the symbol of Alsace's resistance to the German occupier. This most beautiful of villages is full of attractions, including the vestiges of old fortifications, towers, portcullises and machicolations, 14th century churches and 15th and 16th century chapels and wine-producers' houses, not forgetting the château of the Dukes of Wurtemberg, which houses the Musée de l'histoire des PTT d'Alsace (post office museum), the Musée de la Diligence (stagecoach museum) and a micro-brewery. A wine trail leads from the village up through the

vineyards, which include the two Grands Crus, the Schoenbourg, famous for its Riesling, but also giving excellent, long-lived Pinot Gris and Muscat, and the Sporen, planted mainly with Gewurztraminer and Pinot Gris, that produce elegantly full-bodied wines of remarkable longevity.

Grand Cru
Zellenberg

With their heads still ringing from the sound of the fifes from the Ribeauvillé Fiddlers festival (1st Sunday in September), walkers can head to Zellenberg, which in the Middle Ages was named "Little Toledo" due to its unique hilltop defensive setting (285 m). Attractions include a baroque church, built in 1760, a superb view of the plain of Alsace, a history trail and a wine trail. The village has the Froehn Grand Cru, whose clayey marl soil encourages the production of Gewurztraminer, Pinot Gris and Muscat.

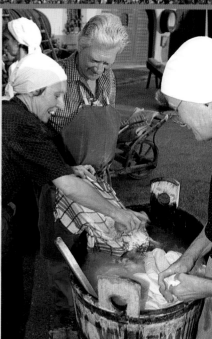

Hunawihr

Hunawihr is easily recognisable from its fortified church and cemetery. The church was built upon a hillock in the middle of the vines, in honour of Ste Hune, a saint venerated by Alsace winemakers. The 14th century tower is decorated with 15th century frescoes that relate the legend of St. Nicholas, the protector of all good children, and the crowning of the Virgin Mary. The local Grand Cru, the

Rosacker, produces full-bodied Rieslings and harmonious Gewurztraminer that should be tasted after a walk round the parc à cigognes (stork park) which, hardly surprisingly, has a number of storks, the emblematic bird of Alsace, as well as otters and a butterfly house. The vine trail is worth the walk, while the local wine festival, the Fête de l'Ami Fritz, is held on the 4th Sunday of August. Hunawihr also produces extremely drinkable Sylvaner and Pinot Blanc.

Ribeauvillé

The three pink sandstone châteaux standing guard over the gates to the village provide a reminder of Ribeauvillé's past, when it was the fief of the counts of Ribeauvillé, right up to the Revolution. A walk above the village takes visitors round the château of St. Uhlrich, with its still partially intact chapel, the Girsberg, more discreet but eternally vigilant and the Ribeaupierre, perched up in the heights. The climb, following the tracks of pilgrims since the 12th century, up to the Capuchin church of Notre Dame de Dusenbach and its chapel is worth the effort. In the village itself, a fountain topped with a statue of a winemaker shows its dependence on the wine industry, while the nearby maison des Ménétriers (fiddlers' house), an elegant 17th century house, boasts an oriel window decorated with a painting of the Annunciation. The church of the Augustine convent, built in 1412, is an excellent example of the architecture of the mendicant orders, and has a splendid double Gothic gate surmounted by a rose window. Building on the St. Gregory parish church, also of Gothic influence, was started in 1282 and finished in 1473. The church houses a magnificent 15th century polychrome wood Virgin with Infant, which is incidentally also the first recorded icono-graphic repre-

A jewel of a town, Ribeauvillé seems to have stayed back in the same era as its three châteaux !

sentation of the ancestral Alsatian headdress. The church also contains one of the oldest organs of the region, the work of Strasbourg organ builder Frédéric Ring. The tour des Bouchers (butchers' tower), the Hôtel de Ville (town hall), built in 1773 and Renaissance houses are the other main sights to be seen when walking around this charming town. Ribeauvillé is also one of the small number of communes with three Grands Crus to its name: the Geisberg, which is partly owned by the nuns of the Divine Providence, gives powerful Rieslings of great finesse while the Osterberg and Kirchberg are renowned for their Pinot-Gris, Gewurztraminer and Muscat. The Clos Zahnacker is a curiosity, producing a wine blended from Riesling, Pinot-Gris, Gewurztraminer and which was first planted back in the 9th century by local monks. Taste the whole range at the local wine festival, held on the penultimate weekend of July.

Not to be missed: The first Sunday in September, the Pfifferdaj, the fifeplayers' day.

Bergheim

Bergheim offers a feast both for the eyes and the taste-buds, starting off with its half-timbered tower gateway, its ramparts and defensive towers, that include the Munitions, the Allumeur (Igniter) and Poudrière (powder magazine), splendid examples of 14th century military architecture. The more sombre Tour de la Sorcière (Witches' Tower) invites you to a closer examination of torture instruments in its museum, open only in Summer. Walk round this lovely village to see the half-timbered houses and geranium and rose-bedecked fountains, before dropping into the Gothic church with its door tympanum decorated with a fine "Adoration of the Magi".

The village has two Grands Crus, the Altenberg and Kanzlerberg, famed for their Riesling and Gewurztraminer, the vines of which can be seen by following the wine trail.

The 14th century gateway leading into Bergheim from the Wine Route.

53

Rorschwihr

Rorschwihr is a village of considerable antiquity, with a tumulus from the Celtic Halstatt era (about 500 BC) and traces of Roman occupation. Winemaking in the village dates back to 742, when the village was recognised for the quality of its wines by the Merovingian Royal Domain, the dynasty that reigned over Alsace at the time. The village's reputation brought a number of sovereigns such as Pépin-le-Bref (Charlemagne's father) and Louis-le-Pieux, along with several Popes and bishops, to own vines within the commune. The village now boasts a 19th century church with the base of a mediaeval belfry/nave.

The village has no Grands crus, but a number of Lieux-Dits.

Grand Cru

Rodern

Rodern was already an important mining village back in the 8th century and has long had a reputation for its excellent Pinot Noir red wine, with its attractive cherry aroma. Rodern's Grand Cru, the Gloeckelberg, has been known since the Middle Ages and now produces Pinot Gris and Gewurztraminer of great finesse and elegance and yet persistent in the mouth. This pretty village has an 18th century church with decorations from the Middle Ages, and a number of houses and courtyards from the 16th and 17th centuries.

Saint-Hippolyte

Saint Hippolyte sits humbly beneath the looming heights of the Haut-Koenigsbourg castle. Its mediaeval ramparts include the tour des Cigognes (Storks' tower), while inside the village are to be found Renaissance and Baroque houses. Founded in the 8th century by Fulrad, Charlemagne's archchaplain, St-Hippolyte is known for its Pinot Noir red wine and also produces a nicely pure, lively Sylvaner with plant aromas. While you are in the village, don't miss the church, built in the 14th and 15th centuries.

Orschwiller

Orschwiller is but a short distance away from two of the finest mediaeval châteaux in Alsace: Haut Koenigsbourg, the magnificently haughty imperial fortress restored between 1901 and 1908, and the Oedenbourg, the ruins of which are in the middle of the forest. In the village itself, visitors can admire the St. Maurice church (1781) and the 15th century houses and tithe courtyard.

The Imperial fortresses

Stern sentries standing guard over the plain of Alsace since the Middle Ages, Haut-Koenigsbourg and Hohlandsbourg are master-pieces of military architecture. The former was restored between 1901 and 1908 at the behest of Kaiser Wilhelm II and its spec-tacular setting makes it one of the essential sights of the region. Hohlandsbourg has also been restored, albeit more recently and in a way that follows the precise plans of the Imperial stronghold, as it was in 1277.

Kintzheim

Sylvaner has made a name for itself in this village, along with some excellent Rieslings. Kintzheim is known for the Volerie des Aigles, with its eagles that swoop down over the heads of the spectators seated within the pink-sandstone castle. The village's other major attractions are the Montagne des Singes (Monkey Mountain), where hundreds of Barbary macaques and apes from the Moroccan Atlas region are allowed to roam freely in the open air, and the Sigoland stork park. There is a yearly wine fair in May, dedicated to St. Urbain, where visitors can taste the Riesling, Gewurztraminer, Pinot Gris and Muscat produced from grapes grown on the siliceous soil of Praelatenberg, the local Grand Cru

Châtenois

Once past the entrances to the valleys of Villé and Argent, under the stern eye of Haut Koenigsbourg, the wine route goes through the town of Châtenois, overlooked by the Hahnenberg, a hill previously covered with horse-chestnut trees. St. George's church is well known for its 18th century

Silbermann organ, and its 12th century Romanesque tower surmounted by a steeple with four bartizans, or watch turrets. The town is the crossing point from the rich, fertile plain of Alsace to the foothills of the Vosges. The remarkable Weingarten Riesling, Pinot Gris and Gewurztraminer should be tasted while you are in Châtenois.

Villé

The nerve-centre of the eponymous valley, Villé is in the heart of orchard country, whence the number of eau-de-vie, or fruit brandy, distillers. The town was founded in 800 and possesses a fine 18th century church. It is the starting point for spectacular hikes over and around the surrounding hills.

Albé

A delightful village nestled between vine and orchard-covered hills, Albé contains some fine half-timbered houses. The annual Summer festival, held on the weekend after the 15th August, shows the eventful history of the village known for its "Rouge d'Albé" and its museum of arts and tradition to be found within the charming Maison du Val de Villé .

Scherwiller

The site of a famous battle fought in 1525 in the shadow of the Ortenberg and Ramstein fortresses, where 25,000 Alsatian peasants were massacred by troops of the Duke of Lorraine, an atrocity that created a deep, long-lasting cleavage between the two regions. Scherwiller and nearby Dambach were the focal points for the Bundschuh peasant uprising that caused the Peasant's War. Scherwiller is a much more peaceful village now, traversed by the river Aubach, that winds by the half-timbered houses, under a multitude of bridges and past wash-houses decorated with a colourful explosion of flowers, reminiscent perhaps of southern Italy. The village holds its wine festival (Arts, Crafts and Riesling) on the third weekend in August and presents its wines to visitors on the Tuesday after 15 July, while a highly popular "gourmet trail" is open on the first Sunday of September. Scherwiller is the commune with the biggest area planted with the Riesling grape and can boast two excellent granite and siliceous lieux-dits, Rittersberg and Ortenberg.

Dieffenthal

Dieffenthal's vineyards are planted round an ancestral "Celtic Rock" and produce an early-picked Pinot Blanc that is considered to herald the start of the grape-picking period in the region.
The village has an interesting 18th century baroque church.

The treasures of Sélestat !

Sélestat is well worth the trip, even if it is slightly off the wine route. This superb historical town contains a number of important architectural gems, including the Romanesque Sainte-Croix church, the Gothic St. George's church, Renaissance buildings (the Commander's Residence) and private houses. The town is perhaps best known for its humanist library, the only one of its kind in the world, dominated by the memory of Beatus Rhenanus and his friend Erasmus. The library contains hundreds of books and manuscripts, including bibles, incunabula and rare codexes, grammar books and learned tomes. The first mentions are to be found here of America and of the Christmas tree tradition ! On the more prosaic side, the Maison du Pain shows the history and techniques of bread-making, illustrated by loaves made in the museum's own, highly-inventive bakery.

Dambach-la-Ville

Overlooked by the protective gaze of the château of Bernstein, Dambach-la-Ville has managed to keep at least part of the wall that protected the town in the Middle Ages, notably against the siege conducted by Armagnac freebooters led by the dauphin of France, the future Louis 11th. The city's three watchtower gateways, dating from the 14th and 15th centuries, lead into the well-preserved town centre, with its market place and the restored 1547 Hotel de Ville (Town Hall) with its timber framing, a Renaissance fountain with its grape-eating bear, the town's emblem, along with some splendid half-timbered houses.

Dambach has the most extensive vineyards in Alsace, which include the Frankstein Grand Cru, best suited to Riesling (delicate and racy) and Gewurztraminer (elegant and floral). Continuing towards the forest, the walker will come upon the Romano-Gothic St. Sebastian chapel, the only surviving building from a village that disappeared in 1285. Inside the chapel, the Gothic nave, lit up at night by strange candlestick arms, harbours a superb wooden baroque altar, sculpted and carved by the Winterhalder brothers in 1690-92. An ossuary outside the chapel contains the remains of some

5,000 peasants massacred at nearby Scherwiller during the Peasants' War.

A wine trail leads through the Frankstein Grand Cru, while the wines can be tasted every second fortnight of April, in the first wine festival of the year, named "Pierres et Vins de Granite" (Granite Wines and Stones) and also on the first Saturday of July on the Nuit du Vin (Night of Wine) and at Eurovin on 14 and 15 August. The commune also produces excellent Auxerrois and a charming Sylvaner.

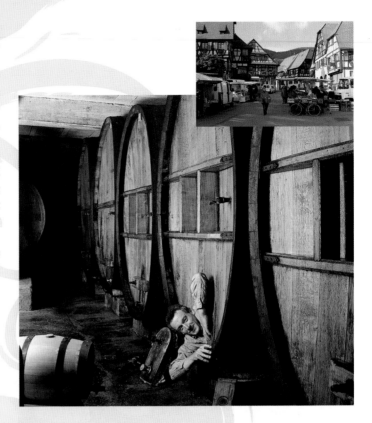

Blienschwiller

A winemaking village since the reign of Charlemagne, Blienschwiller's attractions include a church with a church tower with a Romanesque base (12th century), the 15th century St. Erasmus chapel, a 16th century fountain and a sculpted Mount of Olives. The wine trail leads walkers round the Winzenberg Grand Cru, where the soil is considered ideal for Riesling and Gewurztraminer of some finesse, along with Pinot Gris.

Nothalten

A cosy little village full of delights such as the 16th century fountain and the excellent Muenchberg Grand Cru, capable of producing fat, juicy Rieslings of the highest class.

Epfig

An important winegrowing community, Epfig, like neighbouring Itterswiller, is an ideal introduction to the wine route of Alsace. Once you are off the main road, the village does offer the visitor something to see, notably the Romanesque Ste Marguerite chapel with its Romano-Gothic porch-gallery and ossuary, just by the Fronholz wine trail, that takes walkers up through the vineyards, with a splendid view on the way. The Riesling and Pinot Gris produced from the Fronholtz lieu-dit can bring out the best of the grapes in what tend to be highly individual wines.

Itterswiller

Itterswiller is an utterly charming village running along both sides of an old Roman way, between vine-covered slopes. The village is a succession of hotels, restaurants and richly-decorated half-timbered houses and wine-producers' farms. The local church, with its partially Roman steeple, contains wall paintings of the 13th and 14th centuries.

A Circuit Vins et Gastronomie brings the visitor back to earth via an exceptional view over the surrounding hills and plains. Don't miss the excellent Sylvaners, Pinot Blancs and Rieslings.

Bernardvillé

Nestled in the hollow of a charming valley near the ruins of the 12th century Cistercian Abbey of Baumgarten, Bernardvillé possesses a lovely church with two altarpieces, masterpieces of rococo art.

Reichsfeld

The supposed birthplace of the 16th century humanist and map-maker Matthias Ringmann, who named the American continent in honour of the explorer Amerigo Vespucci, Reichsfeld is a prosperous village lying at the foot of the Ungersberg and possessing a church visited for its baroque statues.

Andlau

Protected by the châteaux of Haut-Andlau and Spesbourg (14th century), Andlau was originally built around the abbey founded in around 880 by Ste Richarde, the disgraced wife of Emperor Charles the Fat. The richly-decorated 11th century abbey-church is a gem of primitive Romanesque architecture, with its crypt, tympanum and historiated frieze showing hunting scenes vying for attention with the stalls emblazoned with the coats of arms of the princess abbesses and nuns who used to live there.

The village itself still has a mediaeval atmosphere, its streets lined with old Alsatian houses with oriel windows and a number of Renaissance buildings, along with an old oil mill that has since been converted into a charming little hotel.

Not to be missed: Wine festival on the first weekend of August, chapter of the Confrérie des Hospitaliers and the fête of Sainte Richarde and her holy bear on the third weekend of September. On the fourth weekend of September, there is a "goutaillon", a guided walk around the Kastelberg, with an open-air meal organised within the vineyard.

The village possesses three Grands Crus: Kastelberg with its mineral soil that can produce some of the very finest Rieslings of the region, Wiebelsberg, also a prime site (siliceous soil) for long-lived, floral Reisling and Moenchberg, well known for its Riesling and Gewurztraminer. The latter, first planted by veterans of the Roman legions, is one of the oldest wine sites in Alsace.

Grand Cru

Eichhoffen

Eichhoffen used to be the village of the abbey of Altdorf and contains the fine 12th and 16th century St John's chapel and an old wash-house. The village shares the Moenchberg Grand Cru with Andlau.

Saint-Pierre

A charming little village, with some fine 18th and 19th century houses, Saint-Pierre also boasts the 12th - 17th century château d'Ittenwiller and a state-of-the-art micro-brewery

Stotzheim

Stotzheim lies on the river Muhlbach and is noted for its 18th century church and the châteaux of Grunstein (16th – 19th century) and Mullenheim (18th century).

Zellwiller

To be visited for its ancient chapel at the entrance to the village and 18th century church with its ossuary.

Mittelbergheim

· · · · · · · · · · · · ·

VINS D'ALSACE

The winemaking village of Mittelbergheim is justly consi-dered as one of the prettiest villages in France and has managed to retain all its rural charm. See the 17th century place de l'Hôtel de Ville, with its Renaissance houses and lanes leading off to the fields

Mittelbergheim is a marvellous reflection of the Alsace of yesteryear.

and vineyards, where all that is missing is the "Ganseliesel", the emblematic little Alsatian girl with her flock of geese, immortalised by Alsatian illustrator and artist Hansi. In homage to the latter, the local wine trail is explained by a strip-cartoon. The wine festival is held on the last weekend in July. The village has its own Grand Cru, the Zotzenberg, which, is famed for making the finest Sylvaner in Alsace, which can now also claim Grand Cru status, the only case of its kind. Excellent Pinot Blanc, Auxerrois, Riesling and Gewurztraminer can also be found here, their character changing according to the vineyards they are grown in.

Barr

Barr's Kirchberg vineyard was elevated to Grand Cru status in 1983 and can produce very fine Gewurztraminer, Riesling and Pinot Gris. The village also boasts four "clos", the Gaensbronnel, renowned for its long-lived Gewurztraminer, the Folie Marco, the Zisser and the Feyel. Barre is a lovely old town of considerable charm, with its Folie Marco museum of Alsatian furniture, that used to be the house of a bailiff. The bailiff was famous for the sumptuous feasts he used to organise before he ended up flat broke, but much appreciated by the townsfolk for his work there. Barr has a wine trail and a wine fair on or around the 14 July, and a Harvest festival on the first weekend of October.

Gertwiller

Gertwiller was mentioned in 1239 in Ste Odile's testament and is today known for its Protestant church with its Romanesque tower and polychrome murals (14th and 15th century). Apart from wine, the village has also managed to win something of a reputation as the capital of Alsatian pain d'épices, a spicy sort of gingerbread.

Heiligenstein

Long protected by the fortress of Landsberg, Heiligenstein is the only site in France where Klevener wine can be made. Klevener, not to be confused with Klevner (Pinot Blanc), produces a spicy, delicately fruity wine, not unlike Gewurztraminer. Also known as Savagnin Rose, the grape was brought in from Burgundy by Ehret Wantz in 1742. The village has a 1558 fountain, with a Merovingian sarcophagus that serves as a trough and a number of fine houses, often with swallows' nests under the eaves. The local fête de Klevener wine festival is in

the second weekend of August.
A wine trail takes visitors on a
walk round the vineyards.

EHRHARD WANTZ
A QUI L'ON DOIT LA CULTURE DU KLEVENER - 1742

DISTINCTION CONQUIT AUX PROGRES

Goxwiller

Goxwiller has a reputation for its Sylvaner and the visitor will see in the village a 16th century wine press and old wells decorated with geraniums, emblematic of Alsace's long love affair with all things growing and flowering. The village also has a fine 12th century Protestant church with a part Romanesque tower.

Bourgheim

Like Goxwiller, Bourgheim has its flower-bedecked wells and visitors can also go round its 18th century church, with its 12th century chancel and belfry and a tympanum symbolising the tree of life. On the wine side, the village is best known for its Sylvaner.

Bernardswiller

A winemakers' village with some Renaissance style wells and some splendid 16th and 18th century houses that reflect the opulence acquired over the generations.

Obernai

Established by the Celts and well-known in Gallo-Roman times, Obernai was first mentioned in a text of 778 at a time when it was called Ehenheim. It was used as a residence by the Hohenstaufens, who, in 1120, built a château there, which was destroyed by the Bishop of Strasbourg in the 13th century. Obernai became an imperial city in the 13th century and, under the astute rule of the City Council, it became an influential member of the Décapole (1354). The town's golden age was in the 15th and 16th centuries, and there are still a number of Renaissance patrician houses to remind us of these past glories. However, decline set in after the Reform, while the ravages of the Thirty Years War brought further unhappiness. Obernai declared its loyalty to Louis XIV in 1679, and its new status of royal town was the sign for prosperity to return. After the French Revolution and the Terror, Obernai entered a new era, with a railway linking it to Strasbourg and opening the way towards a flourishing future, with tourism a major vector in this new economy. Obernai is a magnet for tourists, with a wealth of sights to wander round and enjoy, beginning with the 13th century Kapelturm, or chapel tower, that was used both as a watchtower and as a belfry, and which dominates the town. The Hôtel de Ville (Town Hall) is an eclectic mix of Gothic and neo-Renaissance styles, with a courtroom boasting some splendid painted panels and marquetry showing scenes out of the bible. The Place du Marché is not to be missed, with its fascinating blend of mediaeval, Renaissance, Regency and Louis XIV styles that come together in a

Obernai long had the privilege, come the month of November, of setting the prices of the wine and the wages of the wine workers and to watch over the quality of the local wine production. A wine trail will take visitors all round the town's vines, while offering some superb views of the outlying plain of Alsace and the Vosges. The wine fair is on the weekend nearest the 15 August, while the Fête des Vendanges on the 3rd Sunday in October celebrates the grape harvest. The best-known wines in Obernai are those from the Clos Ste Odile, the Schenkenberg and the Nationalberg, with Riesling and Pinot Gris generally providing the pick of the bunch.

rustic, picturesque jumble that manages to appear extraordinarily harmonious. A winemaking town for over 13 centuries,

Saint-Nabor

A quarry village, St. Nabor contains the remains of the 12th century abbey of Niedermunster and the St. James and St. Nicholas chapels (12th and 19th centuries).

The old abbey of Niedermunster, 2nd half of the 12th century.

The Mont Sainte Odile

The Mont Sainte-Odile has long been one of the most famous landmarks in Alsace. 600 metres up on the Hohenbourg rock, it used to be a holy site even back in Celtic times and is surrounded by a Pagan stone wall, some 10 kilometres long, for which no one has yet come up with an explanation. The convent dates back to the Merovingian era, while Christianity has been a feature of the site since the 9th and 10th centuries. The Mont Sainte-Odile is named after the eponymous saint, the daughter of a 7th century Merovingian noble, and patron saint of Alsace. The miracles recorded around the Saint's sepulchre have been attracting pilgrims ever since the Middle Ages.

Ottrott

Ottrott is at the foot of the Mont Sainte Odile and near the Champ du Feu, a popular skiing spot that overlooks the Bruche valley. The village is pleasant enough and has a number of good hotels. Its attractions include two fortresses, the 12th century Lutzelbourg and the 13th century Rathsamhausen, along with the 18th century château of Windeck, with its English-style park. The Naïades aquarium and vivarium has also proved popular with visitors.

Ottrott has been known for its red wines (made from Pinot Noir) since Mediaeval times.

The Mont Sainte Odile is just nearby, offering some excellent hikes and views. Take a stroll around the Mur Païen (Pagan Wall) that runs round it - the châteaux of Landsberg, Hagelschloss and Dreistein (all within an easy walk of the wall) were built using stones from the wall.

Bœrsch – Saint Léonard

The town of Boersch is surrounded by ramparts and has three impressive fortified gates: Obertor, the upper gate, the Niedertor, the lower gate and the Aftertor, the ramparts gate. The village's ornate 16th century wells are among the finest of all Alsace, while the Town Hall, built in 1617 is a fine example of local architecture. The artist and watercolourist, furniture designer and decorator Charles Spindler (1865-1938) was born in the village.

Bischoffsheim

Situated at the foot of the Bischenberg, a convent with a Gothic chancel (16th century) and remarkable 18th century stations of the cross and nave, Bischoffsheim offers the Sainte-Aurélie church, which dates from the same period and a Renaissance Unterschloss, that is now a farm.

Rosheim

Rosheim is a village with considerable charm, that reflects the whole of the turbulent history of the region. You enter past the remains of the wall that used to run round the town, through the porte Basse (Lower gate) or the porte de la Vierge (Virgin's gate). The village contains the oldest Romanesque house in Alsace, the pink sandstone "Pagan House" and a superb Romanesque church (St Peter and Paul), which was burnt down in 1132 (along with the rest of the village) and rebuilt between 1150

and 1286. The original church was consecrated in 11th century by the Alsatian-born Pope Leo IX. The first fortifications went up in 1213 and Rosheim was made a free town in 1303 and then an Imperial city in 1323, joining the Décapole in 1354. The town grew steadily over the next couple of centuries, and was saved from destruction in the Thirty Years War by Rabbi Joselmann, although it was plundered in 1622 and then again, by the Swedes, in 1632.

The St. Peter and Paul church is typical of the Lombardo-Rhenish style that was the vogue at the time and is built in the shape of a Latin cross, with a sober, even austere exterior. Decorated with arcatures, the church has an octagonal bell-tower with 14th century Gothic mullion windows. A finely-sculpted bestiary, representing the four evangelists, in

the guise of a lion, a bull, an eagle and an angel is worth a good look..

The interior is decorated with yellow sandstone (quarried at Westhoffen) diagonal ribs, pillars and columns, offering a haven of peace.

Rosenwiller

Rosenwiller is home to the oldest Jewish cemetery in Alsace, dating back to the early 14th century and containing some 6740 steles, testimony to the importance of the Jewish community in Alsace. The village also has a church with a chancel, stained-glass windows and wall paintings (14th century) and baroque altars. The wine interest focuses mainly on the South-facing calcareous clay slopes above the village, that produce pleasantly drinkable Pinot Gris, Pinot Blanc and Sylvaner.

Paysages d'hier et d'aujourd'hui

Dorlisheim

Dorlisheim is right next to Molsheim and its main street is lined with a number of splendid old houses and a Renaissance well, testifying to the success of the local wines. St. Laurent's church, built between 1150 and 1160, shows Romanesque and Lombard influences. Note also the 13th century Gothic bell-tower porch, the chancel flanked by two vaulted chapels and the Gothic-style chevet. The village also contains the family-vault of the Bugatti family, the famous car-makers who brought new prosperity to the village in the 20th century. The production line of the new generation of Bugattis is also located by Dorlisheim.

Mutzig

Mutzig used to be fortified, although all that remains is the 14th century gate and was also known throughout the region for its beer and, to perhaps a lesser extent, for its wine. The town contains the former château of the Cardinals of Rohan (17th century) and has a fine Hôtel de Ville (Town Hall) with a belfry and automat, as well as an 18th century synagogue and the Feste Kaiser Wilhelm II, a 19th century German fort.

Molsheim

An ancestral university and Episcopal town, the old part of Molsheim can be entered through the 14th century Forgerons (Blacksmith) gateway. The bishopric of Molsheim was at the height of its influence in the 16th and 17th centuries, when it was the crucible for the Counter-Reform, led by the Jesuits, for whom Molsheim's St. George church was built, with its blend of Gothic and Renaissance influences. The church's architect was a Bavarian, Christopher Wamser and the interior has some fine Baroque decoration.

The Metzig, in the place de l'Hôtel de Ville, was built in 1525 for the Butchers' Guild and is a superb example of Renaissance architecture, like its near neighbour, the Hôtel de Ville (Town Hall) with its gables decorated with volutes.

The Chartreuse (Carthusian) is the town's historical museum.

Built between 1538 and 1792, this former priory now houses the Museum of Art, Archaeology and History and the Bugatti Foundation. Ettore Bugatti, the legendary Italian car manufacturer, set up in Molsheim in 1909 and the extraordinary cars his company produced have made the town famous to car-lovers the world over.

Take a walk along the ramparts to have a view of the Molsheimerberg, the hill containing the Bruderthal, which won Grand Cru status in 1992. The Bruderthal is planted mainly with Riesling, Pinot Gris and Gewurztraminer and its wines can be tasted in the wine fair held every year on 1 May, or at the Grape Festival, the second Sunday of October.

Avolsheim

The wine route winds gently through the countryside to reach Avolsheim, the site of one of the oldest Christian monuments in Alsace, the Dompeter, or Dominus Petri,

to give it its full name. The church was consecrated by the Alsatian Pope, Leo IX in 1049. Just by the village is the Bruche cycle track, a lovely route that runs along the river from Molsheim to Strasbourg.

Wolxheim

The local Grand Cru, the Altenberg de Wolxheim, is noted for its Riesling and Muscat and was supposed to be Napoleon's favourite wine. The village was the birthplace of sculptor Philippe Grass (1801-1876). Visitors can go admire the views along the «Horn» hiking trails, seeing on their way a statue of the Sacred Heart (1912) and the St. Denis chapel standing in the middle of the vines.

The village also has an Alsatian theatre company, with the excellent name of « Les Joyeux Vignerons » (the merry winemakers).

88

Ergersheim

Ergersheim suffered considerable damage during the Second World War and the village's vines are now to be found mainly on the flanks of the Kefferberg hill. The soil is poor and produces dry wines that are typical of the charm and bouquet of the best Alsace whites. Not to be missed is the Notre-Dame d'Altbronn, a Cistercian monastery built in 1895, a fortified farm with a square tower, and the Rimlen chapel, standing in the middle of the vines. The Bruche cycle track runs along the river at the foot of the village.

Soultz-les-Bains

Soultz-les-Bains, as its name would indicate, is a spa village and was renowned for the therapeutic qualities of its waters. Its spa centre, the Sulzbad, was re-opened to the public in 1999. The village is on the Mossig river, which runs into the Bruche canal, built by Vauban, Louis XIV's military architect, for transporting stone to build Strasbourg's fortifications. Wine is produced in the village, while visitors can also enjoy the Jesselsberg hill, opened as a nature reserve in 2002, and the hiking trails that snake out from the village.

Dangolsheim

The Abbey of Schwarzbach in Baden, Germany, mentioned winemaking in Dangolsheim in its documents back in 758. There are two springs, the water from which was already being drunk by the Romans, and which come to the surface near the washhouse, testifying to the rich past of the village. The village church has a part-Romanesque bell-tower dating from 1200 and a Gothic chancel. If you feel like a glass of wine, try the Pinot Gris and the Riesling from the Fürst lieu-dit.

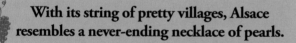

With its string of pretty villages, Alsace resembles a never-ending necklace of pearls.

Grand Cru

Bergbieten

Firmly associated with the Altenberg Grand Cru, which produces some of Alsace's finest Riesling and Gewurztraminer, Bergbieten is typical of Alsatian winemaking villages. The vines here are tended with great care and can be seen by taking the wine trail under the shadow of the remains of the old fortifications.

Balbronn

Balbronn once belonged to the 12th century Holy Roman Emperor, Frederick Barbarossa. Its church houses a replica of the iron hand of Hans of Mittelhausen (16th century), only two examples of which exist in Europe. The village enjoys a micro-climate that makes it ideal for wine-making, fine, complex examples of which are produced from the Weingarten (Riesling) and Hinterkirsch (Gewurztraminer) lieux-dits. The fortified church-tower has an access of a design that cannot be seen anywhere else in Alsace, while the remains of the Romanesque tower of the Knights of Baldeburne are worth a visit, along with the synagogue and the Catholic church with its 15th century tabernacle.

Traenheim

Next to the superbly decorated "Zuem Loejelgücker" auberge, with its 16th century wine-related frescoes, visit the 16th century church with its 12th century tower, 15th and 16th century naves and Merovin- gian sarcophagus. The wine trail will give you an excellent view over the local vineyards, the Couronne d'Or (Golden Crown), so called as they form a crown around the west and south-west of Strasbourg. The Steinecker gives an excellent Riesling, and it is also worth seeking out the wines from the Geiersberg and the Asterberg terroirs, made by two young local producers.

Westhoffen

Westhoffen still has towers and other fortifications belonging to the wall that used to surround the village when it belonged to the Franks. St. Martin's church has a number of attractive 13th century stained glass windows, while the 19th century synagogue has some eastern influences. The village's 8.5 kilometre discovery trail follows a path through the streets, along the vineyards and through orchards and woodland.

Grand Cru

Scharrachbergheim

Borded by the vineyards on the steep western slopes of the Scharrah, the village also has the Süsenberg, a superbly situated vineyard that has had a lot of work done on it to produce the excellent Pinot Gris you can taste in the village. The 15th century Wasserburg, or moated château, with its modern park is worth the visit,

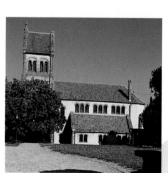

as is the 11th century clocktower and the breathtaking view from up on top of Mont Scharrach (316 metres).

The village also possesses an excellent micro-brewery, one of whose brews is a delightful amber beer.

Dahlenheim

The charming village of Dahlenheim is but one kilometre away from Scharrachbergheim and has a well dating back to 1536. The wine trail is well worth the effort, especially for the view over the plain of Alsace. The village has an excellent reputation for its wine, including the local Engelberg Grand Cru, which is particularly favourable for Riesling and Gewurztraminer. It is little short of amazing how wines of such quality can still be in what could be described as unknown territory.

Osthoffen

Mentioned under its previous name of « Osthova » in 775 in a Carolingian charter, Osthoffen has a church with a Romanesque bell-tower and a 16th century Wasserburg-type château with terraced gardens. The château is privately owned and provides a superb backdrop to the Couronne d'Or wine fair, held there every year in Autumn.

Odratzheim

A church with a 12th century bell-tower and a château dating from 1765 are the main attractions of this small wine-producing village.

Kirchheim

Kirchheim had its period of glory when it was the residence of Merovingian kings Dagobert and Charles the Fat and his saintly, but rejected wife Richarde, who founded the abbey of Andlau. Kirchheim celebrates its past every even year on the third Sunday in July. The village's wine production goes mainly to the local cooperative.

Wangen

Wangen still has remains of its mediaeval fortifications, with ramparts and two watch-towers, including the Nieder-torturm, along with vestiges of an octagonal castle. A wine trail takes the visitor round the local vines, while the local wine festival is held on the Sunday after 2 July.

Nordheim

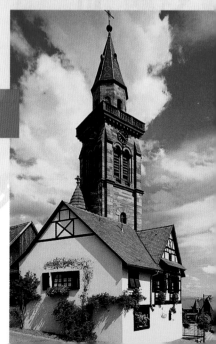

Overlooked by the 372-metre-high Stephansberg hill, Nordheim produces wines of good quality and is certainly the winemaking commune nearest to Strasbourg. Its Gewurztraminer, Pinot Gris and Muscat have well-developed bouquets. The humanist Jean Sturm, the founder of Strasbourg University in the 16th century, went into peaceful retirement in the village. The village has a foot-path that takes walkers to a superb view over the plain of Alsace and the hop-growing area of Kochsberg.

Marlenheim

Marlenheim is the northern gateway to the Wine Route. Its coat-of-arms bears the royal lily, an honour granted by Louis XIV in person. Marlenheim is a lively little town, with a biennial Alsatian book fair, a wine trail, a harvest festival (held every 3rd Sunday in October) and the Wedding of the Ami Fritz, which is acted out every year on the 14 and 15 August, in honour of the hero of Erkmann and Chatrian, the famous Alsatian-Lorraine duo of novelists. Marlenheim was known in the Middle Ages for its red wine, although now Rosé de Marlenheim has taken over, while the village also makes decent Pinot Gris, Riesling, Gewurztraminer and Crémant.

A little gem of a town, Marlenheim's coat-of-arms bears the royal lily

Cleebourg's vineyards are at the northernmost point of the wine route and although they are planted with the classic varieties, Pinot Gris is indisputably the most successful wine made here. The grapes, grown on a rocky volcanic soil, produce crisp wine with a characteristically smoky aroma with lily undertones.

Cleebourg used to belong to the Palatine Zweibrückens and it has a curious history inasmuch as a love story in the 17th century brought it under the Swedish crown. John Casimir von Zweibrücken married Catherine, the daughter of Gustave Adolphus, King of Sweden. The happy couple had a son, Charles Gustave, who, as Charles X, succeeded to the throne of Sweden and thereby also acquired ownership of Cleebourg and its surrounding villages right up to 1787, when Sweden officially renounced its rights to the area, the only vineyards the country possessed!

The village is a quiet place, with some half-timbered winemakers' houses built on sandstone bedrock.

Cleebourg wine cooperative.

Rott

One reason for dropping by this village near Cleebourg is to see the barrel that one-time mayor Louis Andres Rott turned into a bar, engraved with the worthy maxim:

« If you drink, you die, if you don't drink you die, so… ».

Oberhoffen
Steinseltz • Riedseltz

The Cleebourg vineyard is at the northernmost point of the French winemaking area and covers all its communes, as well as Wissembourg, the main town in the canton. It stretches from Rott, with its belfry / clocktower overlooking a cemetery that also doubled up as a defensive hideout in the 18th century, to Riedseltz on the banks of the Rhine. Planted mainly with hybrids or fallen into disuse until the end of the Second World War, the vines were uprooted and the vineyards replanted with the recommended classic Alsace varieties in the 1950's. The local wine producers belong to the Cleebourg cooperative, which has an excellent reputation for all things Pinot, including a blanc de blanc crémant, the "Prince Casimir".

Wissembourg

The town began as a 6th century monastery which later became a Benedictine abbey. Wissembourg has a rich history and traditions that are proudly shown off each year at Pentecost. A town of considerable charm, it used to be home to the Teutonic knights and its old fortifications include two towers, the Husgenossen, or money-changers' tower, completed in 1426 and a square one, built in the 13th century. Walk round the Bruch part of Wissembourg, along the river Lauth, with its allures of little Venice and its old houses. Wissembourg is full of historical buildings, such as the Renaissance houses containing the Westercamp museum, with its treasures of the past and displays of popular traditions. The town's old Dominican convent

was made into a cultural centre by de Gaulle's Minister of Culture, André Malraux, while the St. Peter and Paul church, the second biggest church in Alsace, after Strasbourg cathedral, has some fine frescoes, including a huge, 13-metre high St. Christopher that dates back to the late 14th century. The St. John Protestant church offers a splendid blend of flamboyant Gothic and Romanesque architectural styles.

The Alsace
vineyard

Ideally situated on the protective slopes of the Vosgian foothills, the Alsace vineyard stretches over a ribbon some 120 kms long by 2 to 5 kms wide and at an altitude varying from 180 to 380 metres. Split two-thirds to one-third between the Haut Rhin to the south and the Bas Rhin to the north, the area under vine covers 14,500 ha of mainly chalky ground from Marlenheim at the top, to Thann at the bottom, not forgetting the outpost of Cleebourg at the northern tip of Alsace. Annual production averages out at about 1.1 million hectolitres.

Grape varieties

Alsace has 7 main grape varieties : Sylvaner, Riesling, Pinot Blanc, Muscat d'Alsace, Gewurztraminer, Pinot Gris (also known as Pinot Gris) and Pinot Noir. The wine must be bottled within its terroir, while the name of the grape variety has to appear on the bottle. In 1983 and 1992, fifty grand crus from forty seven sites were elevated to their own Alsace Grand Cru A.O.C.

Sylvaner was first grown on the banks of the Danube and introduced to Alsace by the Austrians in the 16th century. Riesling, was first planted in the region in the 15th century (when it was still part of Germany) and the small, black-dotted grapes are considered by most as the classic Alsace variety, vying with Chardonnay for the title of the world's finest white-wine grape. The Pinot Banc family has two members, the generic version that brought in from Burgundy in the 16th century and Auxerrois, which originated in Lorraine.

There are also two kinds of Muscat: Muscat d'Alsace, which has been used since the Renaissance and the more recently-introduced Muscat Ottonel. Most Muscats are a blend of the two, giving a dry, fruity and highly aromatic wine.

Gewurztraminer has taken over from the old Traminer grape and produces a fruity, spicy wine with a touch of residual sugar, that can be instantly recognisable.

Pinot Gris was first planted in Alsace in the late 17th century and is a pink-tinged, velvety grape that produces a luscious wine, with good acidity and a hint of sweetness.

Pinot Noir, a Burgundy varietal, can be vinified as a red or a rosé wine, with redberry characteristics, notably cherry.

Grand Cru wines indicate the name of the Grand Cru site on their labels, and, with two exceptions, the appellation is restricted to just four varietals: Riesling, Gewurztraminer, Pinot Gris and Muscat.

Late Harvest wines, or vendanges tardives, are made from late-picked grapes harvested in the mists and sun of late autumn. When affected by botrytis, or noble rot, the grapes produce wines of fabulous concentration.

Even more luscious and concentrated, but with a higher potential alcoholic strength, the Séléction de Grains Nobles is produced from botrytis-affected grapes of the same four varietals. These wines are only produced in exceptional years.

The symbols
of the vineyard !

Wine symbols are often seen in Alsace, wherever the winemaker practices his trade. Fixed to the door arches and frames, around the windows and to the corner posts, they vie for space with the equally common religious symbols.

Wine symbols date back to the guilds and mainly consist of pruning-knives, six-pointed stars, the sign of the cosmos and the forthcoming return of the Messiah, and the cooper's hammer, the shape of which is not unreminiscent of a Greek cross and which is normally to be found at the entrance to the cellar, symbolising the birth of the wine, the fruit of human knowledge and the blood of the Son of God. The diamond-shaped form to be found on some window frames refers to fecundity and the shape of the barrels, the bellies containing the living wine. The house is blessed by St. Andrew, the protector of marriage and fecundity, the house and its inhabitants, the cellar and its contents, which makes a quite a job for him. The patron saint of winemakers is St. Urban and every year in Alsace, St. Urban's procession takes place during the Advent festivities around Christmas.

Wine and food

Going along the Wine Route means, of course, a good tasting session but also great food. Alsace is one of the very top gastronomic regions in the country and you can find restaurants serving meals of every style, from farmhouse rustic to three-star gourmet. Here are a few suggestions to help you match the food to the wine.

Gewurztraminer

A Gewurztraminer from a good year is an opulent, spicy wine that will go perfectly with foie gras, munster and other washed-rind cheese, such as livarot, époisses and maroilles. Try it also with desserts such as apple or plum pie, which are generally not too sweet. Drier Gewurztraminers, from a lesser year, will go well with smoked fish, anchovies, sardines in olive oil and herrings in cream, as well as any fish or shellfish served with sauce américaine or with raw ham, such as Parma, Asian food and duck à l'orange.

Pinot Gris

Full-bodied, luscious wines, a Pinot Gris is perfect with foie gras, poultry, white meat and a number of fish dishes. It can also be an excellent accompaniment to ham in a wine sauce, fricassee of chicken, tête de veau (boiled calf head), rabbit in white wine sauce, stuffed breast of veal and roast guinea fowl, and, surprisingly enough, roast lamb. It is also excellent with a large number of cheeses, such as reblochon and mont d'or.

Riesling

Floral, mineral, dry and racy, Riesling reigns supreme over most food from the sea, such as sole Meunière and other grilled or poached fish, fish terrine, shellfish et al. It also provides good drinking with boeuf gros sel, pheasant, goose and duck, and roast knuckle of ham, andouillette sausage, snails, calf-trotter salad (yes, indeed), rabbit paté, ox-tail in jelly, mackerel with white wine and, of course, and who could forget it, the marriage-made-in-heaven of Riesling and choucroute. On the cheese side, dry goat's cheese and mature comté are the best bets.

Sylvaner

A dry, easy-drinking wine, Sylvaner slips down nicely with hors d'œuvre, onion tart, choucroute, charcuterie and fish served in a court-bouillon.

Muscat

Muscat makes for the ideal apéritif and comes to the forefront in Spring where it is one of the very rare wines that can not only hold its own with but also enhance a dish of freshly-cooked asparagus. Try it also with fresh goat's cheese.

Pinot Blanc

The suppleness and discreet fruit aromas of Pinot Blanc make it ideal with all food that is not too spicy, such as terrines, quiche, boudin with apples, tripe, calf's head with gribiche sauce, Alsatian liver quenelles, chicken vol-au-vent, stuffed cabbage, salted turnips and fleischschnacka (a sort of local swiss roll, stuffed with meat).

Pinot Noir

Easy – red meat, jugged game, daube of beef and a good camembert.

Edelzwicker

Made for easy drinking, Edelzwicker is great for picnics, hors d'œuvres such as charcuterie and, of course, tarte flambée…

Crémant d'Alsace

A great aperitif and ideal for receptions, a bubbly Champagne-style wine made for enjoyment, which, at a pinch, will also go with a Camembert.

Fillets of trout served with a crémant sauce and a wild mushroom flan

by Laurent MEISTERMANN, Ribeauvillé.

Wine: Goes perfectly with a Klevener de Heiligenstein or a good Crémant d'Alsace.

Ingredients:

- *2 cooked trout fillets*
- *100 g of wild mushrooms*
- *1 egg, 2 tablespoons of cream*
- *salt, pepper, Cayenne pepper*
- *2 good glasses of Crémant d'Alsace (Alsace sparkling wine)*
- *3 shallots*
- *1 dl of cream*
- *150 g of butter*
- *1 tomato*
- *a pinch of chervil*
- *and ½ clove of garlic.*

Preparation:

Flan: Heat the butter in a saucepan, add 1 diced shallot, the wild mushrooms, salt, pepper, Cayenne pepper and ½ crushed garlic. Sweat the moisture out of the mushrooms, then blend in a mixer Add the egg and the cream, mix everything together well, pour into individual buttered flan moulds and cook in a bain-marie for 20-30 mins.

Sauce: Dice the remaining shallots, add the crémant and reduce. Add the cream and reduce again. Add the butter and mix together well. Pass through a fine sieve, check the seasoning and put aside. Remove the flans from the moulds and place in the middle of each plate. Pour the sauce around the flans and place the two halves of trout on either side. Decorate.

Le Kassler en croûte

Kassler is a slightly smoked fillet of salted pork, and is a local specialty.

by Laurent MEISTERMANN, Ribeauvillé.

Ingredients:

- *1 Kassler of between 800 g and 1 kg*
- *300 g of pork stuffing*
- *500 g of flaky pastry*
- *1 egg*
- *½ glass of Sylvaner*
- *10 unpeeled potatoes,*
- *1 onion, 2 cloves of garlic*
- *1 nice crispy lettuce*
- *1 egg yolk for glazing the pastry.*

Preparation:

Add 1 egg and the ½ glass of Sylvaner to the pork stuffing. Cover the kassler with an even layer of the stuffing. Roll out the flaky pastry, keeping aside a small strip. Place the pastry around the kassler, and seal the edges with the remaining strip of pastry. Mix the egg yolk and brush it over the pastry. Place in a hot oven, cook for 10 minutes and then lower the heat and cook for another hour.

Wine: Excellent with a young, fruity Riesling.

Ox-tail cooked in Pinot Noir

by Laurent MEISTERMANN, Ribeauvillé.

Ingredients (4 people):

- *2 ox-tails, cut at the joints*
- *4 chopped onions*
- *600 g of thinly-sliced carrots*
- *3 cloves*
- *½ a teaspoon of marjoram*
- *1 bay leaf, salt, pepper*
- *1 bottle of Alsace Pinot Noir*
- *1 glass of oil*
- *3 tablespoons of flour*
- *1 litre of beef stock.*

Wine: Alsace Pinot Noir. Choose a deep red wine as opposed to the rosé variety.

Preparation :

Heat the oil in a metal saucepan (preferably cast-iron) and brown the ox-tails. Add the onions and cook gently, adding the flour after a couple of minutes and continue cooking gently, making sure the flour doesn't burn. When the flour begins to go slightly brown, add the wine, stock, bay leaf and marjoram. Bring to the boil, then turn down the heat and leave to simmer for 2 ½ hours, stirring occasionally. Add the carrots and leave to cook for a further 30 minutes. Check the seasoning and then serve with spätzle (a sort of local gnocchi) or mashed potato.

Buying and choosing wine

Choosing the most suitable wine for an occasion sometimes seem like a fairly hazardous exercise to the layman. To make things easier, it is best to stick to a few basic guidelines:

• If you are having a drink at aperitif time, do not forget that you might well be drinking the same wine with the food afterwards, so make sure the two will go together (see the section below on Wine and Food).

• Do not be shy of asking the wine producer or shop assistant for advice - they are there to help you.

• Remember there are some wines to be drunk young (Sylvaner, Pinot Blanc...) but others (Grand Cru wines, especially) that need a bit of ageing. Again, do not be afraid to ask.

• Remember also that good wines are not necessarily great wines, but that great wines must be good wines

Keeping the wine

The temperature of a good cellar should hover around 12° C, with a humidity of 65 – 75%. Lighting should be subdued and the cellar should be ventilated, but without draughts. Wine should be stored alone in the cellar !

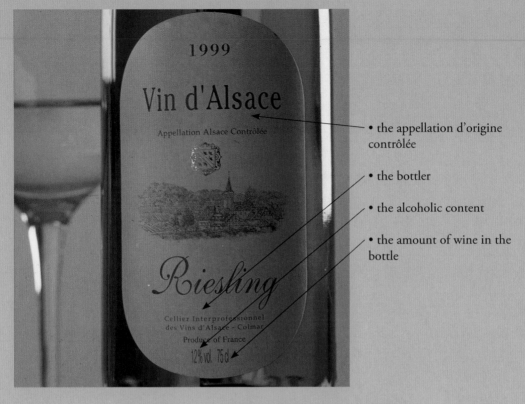

1999

Vin d'Alsace

Appellation Alsace Contrôlée

Riesling

Cellier Interprofessionnel
des Vins d'Alsace - Colmar
Produce of France

12% vol. 75 cl

• the appellation d'origine contrôlée

• the bottler

• the alcoholic content

• the amount of wine in the bottle

Understanding the bottle label

The label on a bottle of Alsace wine must, by law, give the following details:
• the appellation d'origine contrôlée (Vin d'Alsace, Alsace Grand Cru, etc.)
• the amount of wine in the bottle
• the alcoholic content
• the bottler, sometimes indicated by a code-name, but usually by his address. The label should also state whether the bottler is the individual winemaker, a négociant or a cooperative.

Other information which might feature on the label includes:
• réserve, réserve personnelle, cuvée réservée, cuvée X or Y, which have no legal meaning and are more often that not down to the producer's whim
• the vintage, or the year the grapes were harvested.

Glasses and serving temperature

A stemmed glass with an elongated oval bowl, tapering inward at the rim is the kind we are looking for. If you insist on using the traditional glass with its green stem, use the largest one possible. The glass should be filled to between a third and half-way up to allow the aromas to express themselves fully.

<u>Serving temperatures are as follows:</u>
- 6-7° C for Crémant d'Alsace
- 8-10° C for young whites and rosés
- 9-11° C for older whites
- 12-15° C for reds

You can cool the wine down in a fridge, but avoid using the freezer. An ice-bucket is often the best solution, although you should put just enough ice in it to cool the whole of the bottle and not just the bottom third.